Tortoise Taught Us

and other poems

By the same author

'The Pussy's Tail'
ISBN No: 0-9548722-0-7

Tortoise Taught Us

and other poems

Ernest Yelf

Owlprint

Published in 2005 by

Owlprint
PO9 3HE 7

ISBN No: 0-9548722-1-5

A catalogue record of this book can be obtained from the
British Library

Illustrations by Ian Tyrrell © 2005

Printed and bound in Great Britain by
RPM Print & Design
Chichester, West Sussex

For St. Alban's School, without which none of it would have happened.

ACKNOWLEDGEMENTS

A belated very special thank you to Anne for hours of word processing before I mastered the skill for 'Tortoise Taught Us'; for those all important 'first reads' and for her patience when duties of a more practical nature were neglected.

Thank you to Theresa for her always-helpful comments, even when time was pressing.

A special thank you to Catherine for her invaluable, knowledgeable and good humoured policing of my verse and for her forthright championing of correct punctuation. In particular her pleas for more full stops as an aid to the well being of the reader which, perhaps, were neglected by the poet in search of 'higher things'. Nevertheless, I take full responsibility for any errors or occasional loss of breath when reading aloud as I did not always listen.

I should also mention anonymous contributions from the children of Year Four by way of inspiration, unknowingly, they provided for a number of the poems in this book.

Thank you to Lucie, representing the younger reader, for her perceptive observations and courageously for challenging aspects of the poet's logic.

Last but not least, a big thank you to Ian for his artistry and for squeezing a week into forty-eight hours and to Ted for his computer wizardry.

To all the above I am indebted for their time, skills, interest and support, their contributions towards my efforts in writing this book being more valuable to me than they might have imagined.

Contents

INTRODUCTION

It is true that my intention for this second collection of poems primarily is that they be read and enjoyed by children. However, it is not to imply that the enjoyment of nonsense and whimsy is a pleasure exclusively to be experienced by children. If you are an adult reading this, possibly a parent or grandparent or indeed any adult who gained as much pleasure from the book you were reading to a child as the child did from its being read to them, then this book is for you as well. If, however, you are an adult who would like to read it but are embarrassed by the thought of the cover being seen by others, then remove it and replace it with another from a really 'grown up' book of poetry, Andrew Motion's for instance and no one will be the wiser.

I have never believed in 'writing down' to children and within the context of appropriate vocabulary, if a particular word is right for the subject then I will use it. It is my hope that an enthusiastic reader will be sufficiently stimulated to 'look it up'. However, if the book is being enjoyed in a manner remembered from my own childhood, under the bedclothes with a torch for instance, it is asking too much for those cosy confines to be deserted in the name of education and at the same time risk arousing disapproving parents. For this reason I have included at the back of the book, a glossary of words that may be unfamiliar to the younger reader. If it does not include a particular word you are looking for then I am afraid you will have to visit a dictionary.

Ernest Yelf.　August 2005

x

Dancing Lesson

Hey diddle diddle the cat played the fiddle,
The elephant practised her dancing,
An ant that was passing in tutu and pumps,
Made fun of the elephant's prancing.
"How unprofessional, what a display
Of untalented jumping around;
What damage you do to this elegant art,
Not to mention the holes in the ground."

The elephant really was trying *so* hard,
Despite her gargantuan size,
The spiteful remarks from the arrogant ant,
Brought a tear to the elephant's eyes.
The ant didn't care, with her nose in the air,
Flaunted her bold pirouetting,
But to criticise those who are doing their best,
Is unfriendly, unkind and upsetting.

A tap-dancing elephant needs lots of space,
Especially the harder she tries,
So thumbing her nose just in front of its toes,
By the ant was a trifle unwise.

What the elephant did for the sake of her art
Was a private and personal matter,
But she's smiling and there's a new spring in her step
And the ant is *undoubtedly* flatter!

Family Tree

Very, very, very old
Fossils have been found
From before the time when walking
Was the way to move around.
Evolutionary progress
Had just arrived at feet,
Not every prehistoric beast
Had found a way to meet
The challenge of the change involved
When they first discover,
They're going to have to learn to put
One leg before the other.
A defiant little dinosaur,
The fossils' prove it's true,
Had such an awful temper
He was known as 'Angaroo'.
The 'Angaroo' was hopping mad,
His favourite form of movement,
Although he tried he couldn't see
The point of the improvement.
The dinosaurs encouraged him
To change his point of view;
"You can, you can, you can" they roared,
"You can, you can 'garoo".
The dinosaurs were unaware,
Though nothing now could stop it,

They'd just invented 'Kangaroo'
For animals who 'hop it'
But they were very angry
As his method of propulsion
Was delaying evolution,
The punishment, expulsion!
So he was banished to a far off land,
Embarrassed by his failure,
So now you know why Kangaroos
Live mainly in Australia!

One Worm Short

If every worm around the Earth
Decided to reduce its girth
And voted that they all join in,

So every worm would then be thin
And all the worms achieved their goals
Of smart, designer wormy-holes
And then to raise their self-esteem,
For worms are wrongly thought unclean,
They all decide to celebrate
Their fate to be invertebrate,
So to the world they would confirm,
To be dynamic, be a worm!

For a moment just suppose,
From end to end and nose to toes,

They stretched and stretched to reach their limit,
So every worm the Earth had in it,
Made a giant rubber-band
And if, as all the worms had planned,
Around the World they formed a ring,
Apart from one *annoying* thing,
If their plan was one worm short,
And all their efforts came to nought,
Even if they had succeeded,
Would anyone have noticed?

Poet's note:
If you have a pet worm and this poem upset you, I am very sorry.
In fact I think worms are terrific, especially for fishing.

Humpty Dumpty

Humpty Dumpty sat on a wall,
Too high for an egg to be seated,
But his mobile-reception had faded away
And his texting was hardly completed.
Alas for poor Humpty his eggular shape
Was a problem he badly mishandled,
So he rolled off the wall, which was three metres high
And more than his texting was scrambled.

Manners Maketh Mouse

At tea, a pair of furry ears
Appeared between my knees,
To my surprise it was a mouse
Demanding bits of cheese.
The mouse was very bossy,
In fact he asked me twice,
So, just to keep the peace, I thought
I'd spare a tiny slice.
He snatched the piece of Cheddar Cheese,
I'm sure the rodent said,
"Who ever heard of Cheddar Cheese
Without some chunky bread?"
How bad mannered, how ungrateful,
I was only being kind,
The mouse appeared again next day,
Demanding cheese with rind.
He snatched the piece of cheese *again*
And as he left he muttered,
"This cheese is past its 'sell by' date,
This bread's not even buttered".
I'd really had enough of this
And quite enough of that,
If I wasn't so compassionate,
I'd give him to the cat,
But I mustn't be so squeamish,
I must do what I must do,

He doesn't know it but he's bitten
More than he can chew.
"I'm sorry, mouse, the cheese was old,
I'll try a little harder,
Here's a very special cheese,
It's in this sort of, larder".

He snatched the piece of Gorgonzola,
Lying in the trap,

Filled his cheeks and wiped his whiskers,
Burped and that was that.
If you think this is upsetting,
At least his end was snappy
And Gorgonzola guarantees
A mouse expires happy!

If you listened very carefully
To this sorry tale,
You'd notice that the mouse ignored
Some rules that never fail.
The mouse would still be with us,
Enjoying lots of cheese,
If he'd just remembered, *thank you*;
I apologise and *please*!

Birthday Party

Snuggling in my cosy bed,
My teeth are washed my story read,
I've had my kiss and said my prayers,
My daddy tiptoes down the stairs,
He stops and listens, not a 'peep',
As I *pretend* to be asleep.
I've really had so many tries
But I just *cannot* close my eyes,
How can I settle down and rest?
My brain's already up and dressed!
It's not surprising I'm a fidget,
Tomorrow I'm a 'double digit'.

In just four short hours time,
When midnight comes, I won't be nine;

I hope by then I'll be asleep
And trust the 'snuggy' dark to keep
My secret safe 'til morning when,
I'll wake up and at last, I'M TEN!

History Lesson – 1

History books are useful
For telling us our history
But some conclusions they confirm
Remain a total mystery.
Take the case of King Canute,
Who tried to stop the tide,

If proof were needed, this is it,
The history books have lied.

Documents have been unearthed
Beneath an ancient priory,
Amongst the faded manuscripts
Were pages from his diary.
His writing is identified
By those who know much better
And prove that when the writer wrote,
The paper was much wetter.
No further proof is needed
To authenticate the hand,
These *are* the words of King Canute,
With little grains of sand:
"*Went down to the beach today,*
Enjoyed myself a treat,
There's nothing like a wave or two
For cooling tired feet."

Poet's note:
Carbon dating has revealed the diary to be a forgery
and anyway, Biros were not invented until 1944.

Trust

Please help me Mrs. Olive-Jones,
I'm worried and concerned,
The other day you took away
A thing I've always learned
Was to *help* me with my numbers
But you said it would no longer,
Without a thought for my concern,
You took away my comma!
You told us it was optional,
Then said we must not use it,
I'm so confused especially as
It makes no sense to loose it.
I *believe* you Mrs. Olive-Jones,
Every word you say,
So if you *really, really* think,
That taking it away,
Will *help* my understanding then
I'll trust you, just like that
But if, deep down inside, you don't,
Please give my comma back!

Guinea Pig

My doggie is a guinea pig!
I'm in a state of shock,
When I bought him I was certain
He was purebred terrier stock.
The vet assured me it was so
And wrote a new prescription;
"These special pills are just the thing
To cure your dog's affliction.
The medicine's untested",
Said the vet, "but have no fear,
They're very cheap but he *must* take
The tablets for a year".
"We'll start him off on ten a day,
That should cure his trouble
But if you find they've no effect,
Then give the doggie double".
I walked my little doggie home,
His parts seemed in good order,
Flappy ears and 'otter' face,
I'd swear he was a Border.
I've grown accustomed to his 'woofing'
But after fifty weeks,
A shocking truth, the diagnosis;
He doesn't bark, he squeaks!
He's much smaller and much rounder,
His legs are half the size,

A tiny tail and whiskers
And little round, pink eyes.
My doggie *is* a guinea pig!
I'm in a state of shock,
It's clear that when I bought him,
He was *not* pure-terrier stock.

"Your guinea pig's a doggie" said
The vet with great conviction,
"These pills will cure the little chap,
I'll write a new prescription,

Twenty tablets every day,
That should meet the need,
If not then double up the dose,
It's certain to succeed".
At first, no signs of progress,
Of course the vet was right
But it worries me to wake
The little guinea pig at night;
I really have no option,
There is no other way,
To administer his treatment,
Now it's forty pills a day!
A year has passed, the tablets worked,
My doggie reappeared,
I took him to the vet again
And heard what I had feared.
"Your doggie is an elephant",
I was not amused
By his latest diagnosis,
The tablets I refused:
It would be impossible,
To live with it alone,
In the little potting shed
That now I call my home.
Although it seems ungrateful,
At last I've come to see,
My dog was not a guinea pig,
The guinea pig was *me*!

Mary's Lamb

Mary had a little lamb
She loved the lamb 'to pieces':
She fed it, took the lamb for walks
And even wrote a thesis
On varieties of little lambs,
She knew her subject fully,
The trouble was the tale was dull,
Much too long and woolly.

The pieces of her little lamb
She kept inside her freezer,

Each Sunday lunch she chose a piece
Especially to please her.
The lamb was really 'yummy',
It's flavour was the 'tops'
So still she loved her little lamb,
But she *adored* lamb chops.

Tortoise Taught Us

The tortoise's philosophy,
Quite simply put is lowly,
He lives inside a caravan
And travels very slowly.
His funny little bandy legs,
The tortoise will contend,
Provide enough propulsion for
Arriving, in the end!
Efficient use of time is not
The slightest motivation,
For a tortoise to arrive at all
Is cause for celebration.
To this contented quadruped,
That means he has four feet,
A lettuce leaf, a wander and
A snooze and life's complete.
He sets off after breakfast
At eight or nine or ten,
With nowhere in particular
To travel to and then,
When he finds his destination
He meanders back for tea,
As punctual as tortoise can,
At five or four or three.
Prolonged perambulations,
Free of stress and worrying

And tortoise lives one hundred years,
So what's the *point* of hurrying?
Aesop's tortoise taught us,
Most scholars are agreed,
Success does not depend on haste,
For too much haste, less speed.
So pause before you laugh at him,
Reflect before you mock,
The tortoise's unhurried life,
Untroubled by the clock.

My Nose Has Gone

It's 3 o'clock,
My nose is snoring,
The sort of snore
There's no ignoring.
My nose is hurt,
It heard me say,
"I wish my nose
Would go away"
It's 4 o'clock,
There's not a sound
But I was shocked
By what I found;
My nose has gone,
It's disappeared
But even worse
Than I had feared,
As if by some
Hair-raising spell,
All my hair
Has gone as well.
My ears have left
And in their place,
Is just a sort
Of 'eerie' space.
My lips are sealed

And underneath,
There's nothing, where
There should be teeth.
Thank goodness I've
A single eye,
There's little left
To know me by,
Like Cyclops on
A pink balloon;
I hope that I
Will wake up soon!

Haiku: Walking The Dog
in Early June

Leather on willow:
With a satisfying 'thwack'
Summertime is back.

Poet's note:
Haiku is a type of Japanese poetry usually of seventeen syllables, five,
seven, five. The title can be as long as you like. Try some yourself.

25

Nature's Law

There's been a murder in my garden.
I know it's very sordid
But if I'm asked for evidence
The details are recorded,
As I was a witness to
This unexpected killing
And the victim, as you would expect,
Was far from being willing.

I will testify that motive,
As far as I can see,
Was the perpetrator's need for something
Tasty for his tea.

'Not guilty' was the verdict
Nature's law achieved,
Another blow for common sense
But if you have perceived
Injustice for the victim,
I am happy to confirm,
Acquittal for the Blackbird
Was unlucky for the worm!

History Lesson – 2

History books are useful
For telling us our history
But some conclusions they confirm
Remain a total mystery.
Take the case of Alfred,
The king who burnt the cakes,
If proof is needed, this is it,
Of history books' mistakes.

Documents have been unearthed
Beneath an ancient priory,
Amongst the faded manuscripts
Were pages from his diary.
The writing is authentic and
Historians have learnt
From Anglo Saxon recipes,
It wasn't cakes he burnt.
No further proof is needed,
The evidence is glowing,
These *are* the words that Alfred wrote
When outside it was snowing.
"*By (Saxon curse)! it's cold outside,*
There's nothing like roast chestnuts,
Oh (Saxon curse)! I've burnt the lot,
I've ruined all my best nuts!"

Poet's note:
Further research has revealed Alfred's diary to be in the same hand
as King Canute and unlikely to be authentic.

Moonbeam

The moon peeped through the curtains
And shared his friendly light,
To smooth away a teardrop
When I was frightened in the night.
I looked out of the window,
He smiled at me and said,
"The night time will not harm you,
Now tiptoe back to bed".
He kissed me with a moonbeam
And I'm sure I heard him say,
"I will carry you till morning,
When the dark has gone away".

I wipe away the sandman,
The curtains are still drawn,
As bugle calls of sunlight
Are heralding the dawn.
When the sun resumes his duty,
I know the moon's still there,
He's just resting till the night comes,
When he promises to care
For frightened little children,
He will chase their dark away
And carry them on moonbeams,
Until the sun brings back the day.

Flying Poem With Long Words

Aeronautical

      Conundrum

           Indecisive

        Aviator

     Nonsensical

  Illogical

   Airways

       Operator

          Scatterbrained

       Anomalous

    Capricious

   Cabbage

White

   Exasperating

      Inference

     The

        Butterfly

            Is

          Right!

Miss Muffet

Little Miss Muffet sat on a tuffet
Eating a hot 'Peperami'
But the tuffet was not such a well-chosen spot,
It was home to a very large army
Of little red ants enraged when her pants
Invaded their personal spaces,
So they angrily grouped and determinedly trouped
Into all her most tickly places.
"WOW" said Miss Muffet as she leaped from the tuffet,

"The packet said *hot* but not *tickly*",
So she ran to the shop and purchased the lot,
Which she eat quite indecently quickly!

The Special Friend

I've been invited to a party,
The invitation came today,
I was sitting down to breakfast
And I found it tucked away
Underneath the Weetabix,
There was just a corner showing,
I know it's from my special friend
So I am definitely going!

I took it from the envelope,
Being careful not to bend it,
After all the trouble taken
By my special friend to send it
On such very tiny paper
And in even smaller writing,
It said I'd be the *only* one,
My special friend's inviting.

"Stop staring at the table cloth,
Finish up your piece of toast,
We really can't be late again,
We've five minutes at the most.
No you haven't caught another cold,
You were fully fit on Sunday,
It's funny how your colds appear
Like clockwork every Monday!
I know you have a tables' test,
Well, tell your teacher if you worry,
I'm sure she doesn't go too fast,
Now we *really* have to *hurry*".
Why are grownups always rushing?
I need an extra minute,
At school we finish off a test,
Just after we begin it
But I'm going to a party,
After homework, after tea,
I'm looking forward to the party
With my special friend and me.
I'll talk and talk and tell him
All my fears and things I've planned,
He doesn't *care* what time I take,
However long, he'll understand.
Then my 'special' friend will vanish
And he will only reappear,
When he sends an invitation,
Because he knows I need him near.

Grown Up

The emptiness where once you smiled,
The space in which we played,
The hours no longer laughter filled,
By time we are betrayed.
Time cannot erase regret,
Despite the passing years,
For things I did when you annoyed
Like, cutting off your ears
And when you said you thought I was
Not pretty any more,
I covered you in toothpaste and
Stuck you to the floor.

I tried so hard to make amends
By cleaning off the goo
But now I know it wasn't kind,
To flush you down the loo.
Not once did you complain or say
I really was unfair:
I've never found a friend again
Quite like my teddy bear.

If Elephants Were Liquorice

I found the oddest little bottle
Hidden in a drawer,
In a cupboard in the attic
Where I'd never been before.
I was visiting my granny's house,
Exploring nooks and crannies,
Granny's the most curious
Of curiouser grannies.
The drawer was labelled 'private'
And was full of granny's things,
A willow wand and powders
And lots of funny rings
But the bottle was my favourite
And I know to steal is wrong,
So I am only going to borrow it,
I wont keep it for long.

I unscrewed the little bottle top,
The bottle started glowing
And from within its glassy tum
Something started growing.
It swayed as it expanded
And with astonishing contortions
From the bottle grew a genie
Of ridiculous proportions.

As genies go this genie was
A genie who 'had been',
With the largest genie tummy-button
I had ever seen
Protruding from between his ragged
Trousers and his vest,
As genies' go this genie was
Distinctly passed his best.
So this is what my granny had
Been hiding in the attic;
This explains why she became
An Internet fanatic!
She ordered it through e-Bay,
Now I understand,
She only has a pension so
The genie's second hand!

The genie yawned and scratched himself
And when his yawn was through,
Declared in quite unfriendly tones,
"Who, my boy, are you?
You woke me from my well earned rest
You're not my proper master,
I advise you child who let me out,
To put me back, much faster.
I have no time for little boys
Who look in private drawers,
So return me or I'll visit you
And poke around in yours".

Oh crumbs, I thought, I can't have that,
What would my mummy say?
I'll have to find a spell to make
The genie go away.
I read the label on the bottle
And found the perfect spell,
If I said it as I waved the wand
The magic should work well.
Gribbletickypoppletocky
Rubbadubbasear
Point the wand at whom you wish
And they will disappear!
At this very awkward moment
Through the hatch a head appeared,
I recognised the pointed hat
And little wispy beard.
I really love my grandma,
Despite her odd appearance
But sometimes I could do without
My granny's interference.
Concentration's so important,
Take no notice of distractions
When you really need to do your best
And maximise your actions.
So if you bother to do something
Then do it very well,
Especially if you're just about
To say a magic spell!

An accident, I'm sure it was,
It's not the way I chose,
I really didn't mean to point
The wand at granny's nose!
The spell was quite a good one,
The best that I have seen,
There's nothing looking through the hatch
Where granny's head had been
And as if that wasn't bad enough
You won't believe what happened after,
When granny's 'headless' body
Floated up into the rafter,
Then flew around the attic
Like a giant headless bat,
'My goodness, what a clever gran,
How on earth does she do that?'
The head, of course, was still attached,
Just hidden by the spell
But when your head's invisible
It's very hard to tell
In which direction you are flying,
Even genie started shaking,
As she turned and looped the loop
There was no mistaking
Her terminal velocity
As granny's flight was finishing
Ensured a happy outcome for
The genie was diminishing!

I really love my grandma,
Despite her odd appearance
But sometimes I could do without
My granny's interference.
As granny and the angry genie
Wrestled on the floor,
I wished that I had never looked
In granny's private drawer
Because she'd been a grumpy gran
Since she lost her cat
But that's a 'tail' we best forget,
I wont go into that.
I have to find a really super
Multi-purpose spell,
To send the genie back again
And deal with gran as well.
Return the genie to the bottle
And granny to her bed,
Oh and so I don't forget
Give granny back her head.

If elephants were liquorice
With super magic powers
There'd be all sorts of jumbo spells
To practise with for hours
But granny's was a bargain box,
A sort of starter kit,
I've just a single chance to save

My skin and this was it!
I waved the willow wand and said
The spell to work my plan,
Escape from granny's wrath and then
Return where I began.
Gribbletickypoppletocky
Spottalottatwottle
Stuffalottasossajeena
Rubbawottabottel!
Of all of granny's magic spells
This one was a **whopper**,
She moved at such enormous speed
The genie couldn't stop her,
She snatched the genie's trousers off
And vanished in a puff,
He shrank into the bottle top
He'd really had enough.
A genie who is trouser less
Is not a pretty sight
Especially after losing to
A granny in a fight.
I grabbed the genie's bottle,
Returned it to the drawer
Where granny keeps her private things
And closed the cupboard door.

My mummy will be wondering
Why I'm so late for tea,

She'll ask me questions but my granny's
Secret's safe with me.
"Why are you so exhausted Morris?
Why are you so distressed?
It's only half past seven Morris,
Already you're undressed.
You've only been to grandmas,
You can't be worn out sitting
And listening to her stories
As she finishes her knitting."
If knitting is the proper name
For granny's 'starter kit',
I wonder if I say I'm sorry,
She would teach *me* how to knit.

If elephants were liquorice
With super magic powers,
There'd be all sorts of jumbo spells
To practise with for hours
But I only want a small one

Just to play a little joke,
When were doing maths I'll send
My teacher up in smoke.
I'll have to *try* and bring her back
So underneath my pillow,
Of course I'm only borrowing,
The little wand of willow!

$$346 + 289 =$$
$$742 + 336 =$$
$$897 + 242 =$$

A Secret Garden

Wide awake and swiftly creeping,
Mind the creaky bits of floor,
Unsuspecting parents sleeping,
Hold my breath and pass their door.
Down the stairs the carpet hushing
Footsteps keen to tell on me,
Almost there, no need for rushing,
The kitchen clock is striking three.

Whispering of gentle breezes,
Stirrings of a dreaming bird,
Moonlight peeps through trees and teases
Secrets of the sound I heard.
Just one go upon the swing,
Back to bed so no one knows,
Snuggle down and sleep will bring,
Dreams of grass between my toes.

The Munch Box

In the corner of the classroom
Waiting for the bell
Apart from 'tummy rumble' it is
Very hard to tell
From the little coloured boxes
Full of sandwiches and crisps,
A container for a rather *special*
Appetite exists.

Jack has brought a 'munch box', its
Shape is just the same
As an ordinary lunch box
But if you look again,
When pretending not to notice
From the corner of your eye,
I'm sure the box is breathing and
You have to wonder why,
If its purpose is to *carry* lunch
Why does it, underneath
Its brightly coloured little lid,
Have lots of shiny teeth?

Jack says he *made* the 'munch box',
A rather strange invention,
He found the pictures in a book

That Jack had failed to mention
Was all about inventors who
Had clearly not succeeded
And gadgets and contraptions that
Soon were superseded.
On the grounds of health and safety
For a business to survive,
The user must be healthy and
Preferably, alive!
The trouble is he *didn't* read
The reason the device
Was banned because the thing it did
To people wasn't nice.

What is that gooey-chewy sound,
That lippy-smacky squelch,
The lunchy-munchy crunching and
That *terrifying* belch?
Oh dear! Oh my! What shocking taste,
How Grimm, how Swift, surreal;
In thirty seconds Jack became
An 'extra-value' meal.

So let this be a warning to
All children who explore,
Fed up with computer games
And look for something more:
That's fine but if you find a book
With lots of 'fun' constructions,
For goodness sake read what it says
And study the instructions.

The Royal Mail

They've painted the post box a beautiful red:
The one at the end of my road that had faded
To horrible pink, so inappropriate
For the significant job it was doing,
Especially with EIIR on the front.
They've given it back the magnificent, scarlet
Shiny and fresh coat of paint it had lost.
I wonder if they are concerned about e-mail.
I think I'll write more letters!

Jessica's Duck

Jessica, Jessica, a hand if you please,
To cover your mouth when you yawn or you sneeze.
Millions of microbes doctors have found
Are contained in a sneeze so to spread them around
Is unhealthy and selfish so keep them in place,
Inside your mouth, not in some other's face.

Jessica, Jessica *please* heed this warning,
Cover your mouth when you're sneezing or yawning,
The hole in your face is for speaking and eating
With lips at the front for when you're completing
The one or the other, it's only polite,
To keep the inside of your mouth out of sight.

Jessica, Jessica had her own way
And a *very* big yawn but I'm sorry to say,
She paid for not listening with very bad luck,
Into her mouth flew a rather large duck.
It's hard to explain the Aylesbury's choice
But it would not be moved by the small, muffled voice
From under its bottom that's trying to say,
"Will someone please make this fat duck fly away"
But no one could hear her diminishing sound,
Apart from the duck there was no one around

And it didn't speak English so a call of distress,
To a duck is a duck and it couldn't care less.

Jessica, Jessica now it's too late,
Ignoring good manners determined your fate,
If only you'd listened when this poem had started;
Then the duck laid an egg and the poor girl departed.

I Am Not Amused

My pen is poised,
The paper shines
Waiting for
Those clever lines
And witty verse
That trips along,
Well that's the plan
But something's wrong.

I'm not amused,
She's gone away,
At least she left
A note to say
She's gone to cheer up
Andrew 'thing',
You know, the one
The future king
Has asked to be
The 'Royal Rhymer';
She really is
A social climber.

I'm not amused,
And neither's he
As he finds

His poetry,
Carefully crafted
Every time,
Keeps ending in
A funny rhyme.
He'll soon discover
Every day
Her whisperings
Have led astray
His poetry
Of fine repute;
She'll earn the 'Order
Of the Boot'!

I'm not amused,
I have no choice
Since I've lost
Her tiny voice
That whispered nonsense
In my ear,
The gift to poets,
An 'idèa';

Until I welcome
Back my muse
I'll put my pen
Away and ... snooze!

Poet's note:
Andrew Motion is the Poet Laureate: a very serious poet.

The End?

This poem you're reading
Is last in the book,
All I have written are read,
But if you are planning
To start from the back,
The end is beginning instead!

Poet's note:
This was written without the help of a muse.

Glossary

acquittal: To be freed from a charge by being found not guilty.

administer: To provide or apply a remedy or cure for something.

aeronautical: To do with flying or travelling in the air.

Aesop: A Greek writer who lived in the sixth century B.C. He is famous for his short stories or Aesop's Fables as they became known. His characters were often animals, their tales conveying what he believed to be truths or wisdom. One of the most famous is The Tortoise and the Hare.

affliction: Distress caused by illness.

anomalous: Irregular or abnormal.

arrogant: A very assertive or bossy attitude.

authenticate: To establish the truth.

aviator: A male or female flyer.

Aylesbury: A breed of large white duck.

betrayed: To be let down in the context of trust.

capricious: Unpredictable or whimsical changes of mind or behaviour.

carbon dating: A method of finding out the age of certain very old objects.

compassionate: To be sympathetic or pitying of someone or something.

conclusions: Results reached by reasoning.

contend: To state clearly or maintain an opinion.

contortions: A twisting of the body or face.

conundrum: A riddle or puzzle.

conviction: A firm belief or opinion.

crafted: Skilfully put together.

curious: Strange, surprising or odd.

Cyclops: In Greek mythology, a legendary giant with one eye.

defiant: Openly disobedient.

diagnosis: The identification of a disease by means of the patient's symptoms.

diminishing: Becoming smaller.

dynamic: Powerful, energetic, active.

eggular: Egg like. (*This word is not in the dictionary but it should be.*)

evolutionary: To do with the process by which a species develops from another.

exasperating: Intensely irritating or infuriating.

expulsion: To be forced out.

flaunted: Showing off in an undignified manner.

gargantuan: Enormous or gigantic.

glossary: An alphabetical list of words with explanations relating to specific subjects or text.

girth: The measurement around the waist.

Gribbletickypoppletockyrubbadubbasear: A very powerful magic spell to be used with caution.

Gribbletickypoppletockyspottalottatwottlestuffalott asossajeenarubbawottabottel: A very, very powerful magic spell only to be used in the most extreme and desperate circumstances. (*It's quite safe to say these spells because they won't work anyway without the little willow wand which I have hidden in a secret place for my own use.*)

heralding: Announcing the approach of something.

hushing: Making silent or quiet. (*This word is not in the dictionary but it should be.*)

illogical: Without any reasoned thinking.

inappropriate: Not suitable.

indecisive: Hesitating.

inference: A conclusion formed from facts or reasoning.

invertebrate: Not having a backbone.

manuscripts: Books or documents written by hand.

meanders: Wanders around at random.

microbes: Minute living beings; bacteria, causing disease. (*A very sensible reason for always washing your hands with soap before a meal.*)

mishandled: Dealt with incorrectly.

motivation: Something that has persuaded a person to act in a particular way.

multi-purpose: Having several purposes or intentions.

muse: Based on Greek and Roman mythology, an imaginary goddess who inspires creativity in a poet.

nonsensical: Amusing by being illogical or absurd, especially in literature or poetry.

operator: A person who works or controls skilfully. (*I know a butterfly is not a person but you know what I mean.*)

Order of the Boot: An informal phrase meaning to lose a job or more specifically, to be 'fired'.

perambulations: Walking about or from place to place.

perceived: Understood.

perpetrator: Somebody who has committed a crime or something outrageous.

philosophy: A belief reached by the use of reason and argument in seeking truth and knowledge of reality.

pirouetting: Dancing on one foot or the point of the toe.

prancing: Raising the front legs and springing from the rear legs. (*In the elephant's case, used to describe her attempts at dancing.*)

proportions: Size or dimensions.

propulsion: The act of pushing or moving forward.

prottle: *(A completely unknown word but I thought you might like it to use when you can't think of anything else.)*

pumps: Light shoes for dancing; would be used by a ballet dancer.

punctual: Arriving on time; neither early or late.

repute: Reputation, or what is generally believed or said of a person's or thing's character or standing.

rind: The tough outer layer on a cheese.

Saxon curse: A very rude word said in moments of stress.

scatterbrained: Disorganised thought through lack of concentration.

significant: Important.

snuggy: Protecting and comforting. (*This word is not in the dictionary but it should be.*)

squeamish: Easily feels disgusted or sick.

surreal: Strange or unnatural.

terminal velocity: The maximum speed of a falling body that the resistance of the air will allow. (*Sorry this is so complicated; ask your teacher to explain.*)

testify: Give evidence, normally in a court of law.

thesis: A detailed written work on a particular subject.

tutu: A ballet dancer's short skirt of stiffened projecting frills.

verdict: A decision or judgement in a court of law.

whiffly: A rather horrid way some children answer back their parents or teacher, without actually saying anything.

whimsy: Playfully unusual or attractively odd humour.

wrath: Extreme anger.

Poet's note:
The definitions in this glossary emphasise the meaning relevant to the poem in which they are used. However some words may have a broader or even different meaning in another context and a dictionary should be consulted in those circumstances.

Dear Muse,
Please come back, I have had to
finish this book early since you left.
What have I done to upset you?
I have tried not to write any rude poems
and I have mentioned 'bottom' only once.
Was it something to do with…?